T0208844

Broken
to be
Triumphant

A book of Poetry

Carl Todd

authorHOUSE®

AuthorHouse™
1663 Liberty Drive
Bloomington, IN 47403
www.authorhouse.com
Phone: 1 (800) 839-8640

Published by AuthorHouse   04/01/2015

ISBN: 978-1-5049-0165-9 (sc)
ISBN: 978-1-5049-0249-6 (e)

Library of Congress Control Number: 2015904382

Photograph Listing

Poem Listing

Opening Thoughts

May you be lifted spiritually into God's hand and empowered to walk on the path He set before you. Along the way, accept whatever you're given and He will bless you. Let go of words that bind you. Listen to your inner voice and never allow your life to be less because someone said it should be.

A Mirror
Sunday, March 1, 2015

A mirror to our face
Flat against the wall
Framed and elegant
It reflects our soul
To see a truth
Darkness and light
Above and below
See how
Retracting the compass
Detailing life
Our imprint
Its time
Ancient and lovely
Set upon a page
Many names
Across the flat plane
We tend to rhyme
Our endlessness
See how it's etched to disc
Black and round
Spinning on a phonograph
Yet flawed in relentless mass we keep
It spins at a different speed
For everyone a reflection
Upon the glass
Framed and elegant
Reflects who we are

Dedication Page

To my sister Georgeanne, the anchor in my life and the touchstone I trust. You are my best friend who never failing to be anything less than that.

To my Aunt who never lost sight of my talents. She became my proof that anything is possible. Whatever life dishes out can be overcome with faith. Push on, push on!

To my mother, precious and dear to me, I have made this journey because she is strong, resilient and a pillar set before me by God. By her example I set my own life.

To the rest of my family who quietly surround me with applause and encouragement to press on: so I do.

My friend, wherever you might be. My love for you has never faded and never failed. Together, our friendship felt like magic in the many talks we've had and the music we created. A true talent, the son I never had; having the privilege to co-share parenting, mentoring and then, above all a brother in Christ you became.

You are the color of light and a beautiful soul!

To Walter, I dedicate the volume of this work.

Thank You,
Carl

A Box Called Time

Thursday, March 7, 2013
Carl Todd

If only I had the time
To walk each day
With you beside me
Beneath the stars
I would hold your hand
And call you my own
If only I had the time
To walk with you

If there was a way
To build a box
Called time
With a seal upon its seam
Your name it would bare
If I could I would
Place it in this box
Called time

If I could create
A flower bed for you
Every peddle; every color
Would be for you
If I could I would
Keep you here with me
Forever as the Milky Way
And the stars that live there

If there was a way
To build a box
Called time

All the hours and minutes
Meld together as one
If I could I would
Place it in this box
Called time

Daddy

Sunday, May 1, 2011

A light shines, no one else can see
A voice heard, no one else can hear
A smile comforting and good
A hand never parting
Laughter of honesty
Never forgotten
Remembering a heartbeat
Holding close the one you love

You are a beacon within me
A touchstone always near
My strength, my friend
My all in all

Daddy

Angel's Among Us

Tuesday, December 24, 2013

There in silence
Darkness falls
There in its fault
A light comes forth
Guiding anyone who sees
Inside peace dwells
A flawless beating
The heart of all
Leading us forward
Through doors on earth
Floors paved
Crossing borders
O' glorious splendor
A home beyond our call
Time endless and bound
There in silence
None can forget
Sounding songs of joy
Surrounds every soul
Look a window opens
There and here
Among us angels
O' beauty in light
Running to catch
Anyone who falls

Destiny

March 1, 2014

Ghostly silhouette
Who is this I see
Moving alongside me
A nameless shape
Why haunt me
Then I hear you speak
I'll be your desire
Calling to you
Wanting you
I'm the second beat
In rhythm with your heart
In my rearview mirror
A glimpse I see
Warm loving eyes
Is it you
Whispering my name
Why haunt me
Then I hear you speak
Come with me
Dance with me
Touch me
I'm the second beat
In rhythm with your heart
Yes its me
There's a chill
If I dare say
I know your name
Its locked away
The key you have it
I'm ready, turn me now
Then I hear you speak

Eternity
One life, one time
Never look back
Never worry
Move without regret
Yes its me
My name is Destiny

Double Edged Sword

Sunday, December 30, 2012

Tilt back your head in a state of rapture
Your eyes lifting to meet the sky
In one breathe we cry out
In hope we're heard
By the God of all

Double edged sword
Wielded by He
A truth of fire yea, cutting deep
Lies abated and uncovered
All will see a double edged sword
Falling on thee

God walking beside us
Unheard footsteps
Never doubt, never second guess
Raise your voice, open your hands
Let's praise Him

Double edged sword
Face to face you will meet
Its mirrored finish,
O' brightest glory breaking through
His conscience searing
Words of power

A double edged sword
Always present and right
Always strong and guiding
Always teaching by a fire and truth

Drop

Saturday, January 24, 2015

Wind my body holds, the floor a cloud
Shadow seen, a landscape below
Decree of God, His splendor an abode
Beyond the gate, set between here and there

In time released am I
Dropped gently, a passing sound above
Thunder sounds I fall
Lightening shows the way
Into the city of choice
Delivered by the invisible hand

Soft is my landing, merged with many
We're moved along, in a rush
Along a yellow painted curb
Together as one into a drain
Curved then straight
Beneath the streets

Destination a great plain
Created to be part of all
Above and below I'm a drop of rain
A tear from the sky, now part of the sea
Yet, for awhile

In the process I'm lifted
Once again to live
Wind my body holds
In the arms of He
The One who controls

Echo of Time

Monday, October 15, 2007

Here in this place
I've come to observe
Stilled in time
Dancing clouds
In one, then two
Combined with blue
A veil behind
Somewhere beyond
A distant song
Rising with the sun
To the beat of a drum
Moving shadows we see
Her mountains
Listen...
Whispering secrets
Never told
Of age and stone
She is the echo
The echo of time

Let Me Be A Vessel

Monday, November 26, 2012

I've been trapped in a prison
Forty years defeated
A child lost
One act of violence
Broken to be triumphant
Frozen to the face
A clock stilled
Marks the flight
A moment of descent
Into the unknown
I was cast
Without sight
The ability to grasp
Broken I stood up
To catch a ray of light
To understand or make sense of it
Sealed in silence, there the child slept
Grievous, was my spirit
I can't describe
Broken I'm built strong
Through a swinging door
A messenger the child received
Stirred by its wake
A ripple against the tide
A child awakened
By a spirit he sees moving freely
He rose to the surface, needing to reach
A new day for the child once lost
Freed from a silent grave
Let me be a vessel
Broken I rose healed

To say what needs to be said
To any child whose been lost
No act of violence can hold you now
Everyone has a messenger
Someone sent with a key
To the vessel, you are now free

Lifted

Saturday, August 30, 2014

I'm a story in a book
Taking you with me
High above the sea
Cliffs support my feet
A canopy of trees
Stretched before me
A flying carpet
Stitched and woven
Beneath my feet
Waving in the wind
O' joyous ride
A song sung on high
Freedom of spirit
Lifted beyond the stars
Just let it ride
I'm a story in a book
Somewhere distant
A land set over deserts
Mountains rising
Meeting the sun
My home is found
Written on paper
I'm bound
For centuries to come
A precious map to be
O' joyous ride
A song sung on high
Freedom of spirit
Lifted beyond the stars
Just let it ride
For the one who sees

For the one who hears
I'm the keep
The key to inner peace
Your journey
Through each page

Love Can Be Silent

Tuesday, December 25, 2012

Love can be silent
In the flight
Of a butterfly
Gliding on the wind
Catching a child's eye
Watch them run
Chasing their imagination
With stretched out arms
Wanting to fly
As the butterfly
Love can be silent
Beneath the sun
Reaching into the ground
Urging life to come
In blooming flowers
Their sent fills the air
Embracing spring
In the early dew
Dripping from pedals
O' their splendor
Love can be silent
In a heart, in a song
Love can be silent
In a poem, in a smile
In arms open wide
Love can be silent
In a spirit unseen
Love can be silent
In all its glory, waiting
Not wanting silence
O' lovely heart to bear

Never let silence calm
O' lovely spirit to share
Never ignore a caring soul
O' lovely silent love
Shout it, let it out today
O' lovely silent love
In a joyful sound
O' lovely silent love
Be heard, be loud, be strong

O' Lovely (My Joy)

Saturday, February 14, 2015

Your smile
Bright shining light
Beauty in the night
Wondering thought
Dancing image
You haunt me

Rooted deep faith
Courageous spirit
You've run the race
Against the odds
You have won
Our beacon of hope

O' lovely…my joy
Come to me

War in a world
Arrow of poison
Racing to end
Forever this mortal coil
A spinning coin
Our silver cord

O' lovely…my joy
Healer…my keep
Come now, come to me

I'm faltered
Can't live
Can't move

Can't walk
Paralyzed by a kiss
I'm drawn
I'm fallen
I'm lost
Are you a ghost
In my mind

O' lovely…my joy
Healer…my keep
Come to me

Pretty Eagle

Wednesday, April 30, 2014

Pretty eagle
In the sky
A quiet cry
No one hears
Just a blue ceiling above
And the earth below
She glides
Through the air
Her shadow touching earth
A seamless line
She holds
Without hands
No walls around
No cares at all
O' beauty on high
To admire you
Captured by all
You inspire
You bring joy
You bring us awe
Pretty eagle
In flight
Moving into the horizon
You disappear
From our sight
Your image left
A picture eternal
O' beauty on high
Forever in our heart
A song born

Simple and true
We look for you
Pretty eagle
In the sky

Pretty Little Angel

Saturday, May 18, 2013

Angel, pretty little angel
With your golden hair
Colored by the sun

Angel, pretty little angel
A beautiful smile
God's gift given to us

Angel, pretty little angel
Running like the wind
O' joyful joyous spirit

Angel, pretty little angel
Laughter sings to my heart
A special name given

Angel, pretty little angel
God's pretty little flower

Resolve - Act - Move

Wednesday, March 13, 2013

Come with me
Leave pain behind
Take my hand
You will stand
In power your fit
Run like the wind

Resolve it now
Don't worry 'bout tomorrow
Act now walk through it
Don't listen to fear and doubt
Move forward
Don't worry about yesterday
Resolve...act and move

Trust my heart
Little lamb don't cry
I'm strong and able
Receive my spirit
Each step restored
I'm with you

Resolve it now
Don't worry 'bout tomorrow
Act now walk through it
Don't listen to fear and doubt
Move forward
Don't worry 'bout yesterday

Along the way
You will stumble
The path is cluttered
I'm able to clear it
Keep in step
Tomorrow's a new day

So Many Words

Saturday, March 29, 2014

So many words
Refreshed you my soul
So many words
Refreshed you my life
So many words
Refreshed you my lips
Along the shore
I spend with you
Recorded in time
In the abyss of the sea
I cannot see
I cannot know
This new beginning
I've been given with you
So many words
Refreshed you my soul
So many words
Refreshed you my life
So many words
Refreshed you my lips
In the distance
Cradled and safe
Two become one
A song emits
Haunting buoy
Echoes infinity
New lyrics in a song
Born to be
To be with you

Tears of the Lost

Wednesday, October 23, 2013

Innocent child suddenly taken
No words to speak
A woman bows her head
A movement of solace
Mommy weeps, her cup
O' see it filled, endlessly torn
No reason, no answer
No time is left, a broken heart
A crippled moment

Let us gather now all the tears
All the sorrows, all the names
Into one place
We bind by sand and stone
A depth beyond the eye
A plain beneath the deep

From a distance one man, a father
A face now covered
With trembling hands, no control
A loss of love one precious soul
Now waves upon the sand
Tenderness there we see
Hand in hand together we walk
No religion, no race, no meaningless words

Let us gather now and take our place
Along its shore a sea of love
Note its peace, note its quiet splendor
Hush now child, our little ones
The tears of the lost
No age at all

The Aging Sun

Monday, March 2, 2015

Through an open door
Two steps
One movement
Beneath your rays
Into the arms
Above, beyond
O' great void

Like a feather
Floating
You embraced me
Filled with sweet splendor
I cannot control
How to conceive
Or be known
All is found
Pictured in a sky
Placed in the deep
Her bosom
To cradle and keep

O' thou
Star in the night
Your fanciful dance
A mirage
A caress of warmth
Lifted from the desert
Played with vigor
Pallet rich, I see a painter
Full of vision
A brush moves

The sand blows
Flawlessly in motion
A captured snapshot
Forged to display
The aging sun
Graced and eternal

The Cup

Wednesday, May 1, 2013

In a world filled with want
Racing hearts beat
Rivers of blood unseen
In rhythm with ocean and sea
Waves moving as restless giants
Wanting more sand
Foreign labor, see tiny hands
A workforce; Woe, little they have
All nations scrambling to own
No thought to their empty cup
All the stuff dragging drapes
Collecting dust
Crowds gathering, heads down
Eyes glued to a lighted screen
Fingers moving to and fro
There's silence
Letting someone know
A position held in line
Floating in cyberspace
Chatter dwells
Grabbing at its hem,
Not seeing tears of a child
Something new in hand
Nations smile
Wanting, needing, it is greed
Clamoring stampedes, a rush to get
As doors open wide
Scrambling in mob filled malls
Crying if there's nothing left
Emptied wallets, flooded credit cards
For what?
An empty cup!

The Table Set

Tuesday, November 27, 2012

Four legs, four chairs
Freedom to add more
A flat round surface, finished wood
A place to sit everyday
It supports, it delivers, it nourishes
It gathers together families
It creates lasting friendships
It gathers our tears
Yes, a place to cry
A place to sigh
It reveals our soul
It reveals our heart
It's a place to join hands
It's a place we pray
It's a place of grace
Four legs, four chairs
Freedom to add more
A flat round surface, finished wood
A center piece of grandeur
A foundation never broken
Worn by constant use
It's sound in character
By memories it reveals
It's comfort when it serves
It's a cornerstone of victory
It's where we are grounded
A place to contemplate
A place to decide
A place that's quiet
A place we can love

The table's set best
When it's bare and clear
Defined by a centerpiece
Our Lord and Savior

Tremble

May 10, 2005

My love for you
I can't explain
My love for you
Soft as summer rain
My love for you
Its steady rhythm
My love for you
Reaches to the sky

My love for you
Makes my heart tremble
The darkest hour
I'm bathed in moonlight
The beat of you heart
With mine...
Its thunder passes over

My love for
A pillar of stone
My love for you
Never fails to prove
This life is but a moment
In time standing still
That we walk through

My love for you
Makes my heart tremble
Like the strings
Touched by a bow
Vibration of a Cello
Makes our souls one

The trembling heart
It will never fail
No matter what comes
Bound by it
Yes forever

Together

November 27, 2014

Can't live, Can't walk
Without you, my love
Can't live, Can't walk
Without you I'm lost
Without you, my love

I'm a frame without a portrait
Setting on a table in a corner
Sunlight casting her shadows
Dancing around me
The curtain billowing
Caught in a breeze
Inside a room alone
Needing someone to hold
In this moment watching
The hands of a clock
Moving me forward it cannot stop
The age of it all
On the mantel in the distance
I see it, I speak it

The story yet be told
I traveled far in a box
From sea to sea I'm here
One beginning one end
A portrait in someone's head
Ready am I to receive
The joy of life
I'm entrusted to hold
I'm entrusted to care

A memory
To be framed
In suspended time
With me

Can't live, Can't walk
Without you, my love
Can't live, Can't walk
Without you, I'm lost
Without you, my love

Forever and constant
I am here
A frame to hold you upright
Together on this table
Living this one life

To Honor Him

Saturday, December 6, 2014

In this place I stand
The darkened hall
Filled with love
A staircase round
Every level of seats align
Straight rows ready
For the many flowing in

The quiet before one note
Movement in the pit below
Intensity calls to me
From beyond these walls
The curtain is drawn
One single candle lit
Yea, to honor Him

The first breath
My soul shaken by the roar
In the dark illuminated
I stand in its presence
And then…..

One violin to bring me in

Our Father beneath the dome
Hallowed be Thy name
A kingdom come, one Will is done
On earth and heaven above

Everyone beneath
Now they stand
Man, woman and child
In beautiful tones
Together we sing
The orchestra begins

In full and glorious voice
A heavenly Choir
Brings the house before His face

For there is power
There is peace
There is glory
Forever. -- Amen.

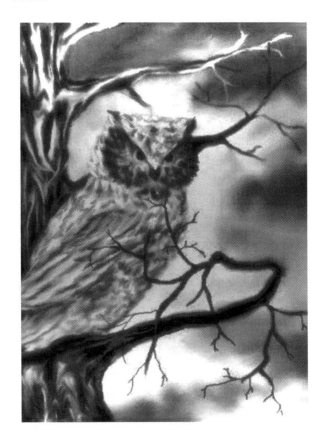

Unseen (Drop reprise)

Saturday, January 24, 2015

Wind my body holds
The floor a cloud
Shadow seen
A landscape below
Decree of God
His splendor an abode
Beyond the gate
Set between here and there

In time released am I
Dropped gently
A passing sound from above
Thunder calls
I fall
Lightening shows the way
Into the city of choice
Delivered by He
Unseen

Soft is my landing
Merged with many
We're moved along
In a rush
Along a yellow painted curb
Together as one
Into a drain
Curved then straight
Beneath the streets

Destination a great plain
Created to be part of all
Above and below
I'm a drop of rain
A tear from the sky
Now part of the sea
Yet, for awhile

In procession, I'm lifted
Once again to live
Wind my body holds
In the arms of He
The unseen

The Original Manuscript
The Aging Sun

Wednesday, March 2, 1988

I lived in Lancaster County at the tender age of 25. Looking out the third floor window (glass designed in 1800). I wonder how many eyes have seen this view. Listening to Mortal Coil's "It'll End In Tears."

Through an open door....picture a sky of the deepest blue. And visible only for a moment on the horizon a fading moon...that soon passes from view. Behind a mountain shadowed by dawns twilight. Reflecting from a lake, like a mighty castle. See the trees reaching like a million fingers to the height of one bird in flight. Through the open door, watch the leaves as they dance in the wind without a care. Then feel the warmth of the air as the aging sun slowly rises from her sleep. Once cradled in heaven, she has many stories to tell. Some good, some bad. Anger, hate, love and peace she told. Only the stars and moon will hear in the endless rhythm of time, it moves to the speed of light reaching this tiny planet to warm us. Standing at the door and looking onward wanting, needing more....yes even more.

My Friend

Wednesday, February 24, 1988

I've been dreaming of you
My friend, the years yet few
I fondly remember

In you I saw the beauty, yes silent love
It was never spoken of

In all of it, a wave lifting me up
You carried me across
A place I was lost
I couldn't see without you

Through you my friend
My life has been blessed
Inspired to dream
Inspired to live it

Sleep

Monday, December 15, 1986

Sleep
Sleep

Come rest your weary head
Whispered secrets no one hears

Sleep
Sleep

Golden wheat sways on the dreamscape
Dandelions white and blowing in the wind

Sleep
Sleep

A twitch upon the sheet
Someone you meet in the dream

The Bridge

Sunday, July 26, 2012

Board by board
Cut and hewn
Laid together
Across the abyss
Nail by nail
Held together
Unconditional love
No power can undo
But made clear
Something strong
Stripe by stripe
Not one less
Not one more
The day was set
He built a bridge

The Pond

The quiet of a pond
Her borders embrace its life
The serenity of its movement

A Sonata in the works
Each note touched by God
Bound by the line of her shores

She speaks the language of time,
Eons old, a beautiful story I behold

The quiet of a pond
The quiet of the Lord
The silence of her soul